Take-Home Cards are also available for friendly prompts and suggestions for parents reading with their children. You can store the relevant card with each book in your 'Take-Home' selection of titles.

Reading skills

Stage 6 develops:

- strategies for independent reading, including consolidation of irregular phonological and spelling patterns
- insights into feelings and motivation of characters
- a wider sight vocabulary
- awareness of other viewpoints
- confidence through familiarity with the characters and the format
- sustained independent writing.

Vocabulary chart

A Fright in the Night	Year 2 High frequency words	an be but by called came do don't door from good got had have her home house laugh(ed) little made make new nine not off old one out over pull(ed) put ran saw seen so some take that there time too took two very water were where will with
	Context words	blackberries downstairs fireplace ghosts haunted heard joke labels monsters noise plastic sheet such switched things toast torch worry
Rotten Apples	Year 2 High frequency words	about after all an but by called came did down from good got had help her his jump laugh made off out people put ran red saw so some then took were what with
	Context words	bought cheap drunk dustbin empty faster funny heavy noise present reins rotten slow sold sorry sway things turn
The Laughing Princess	Year 2 High frequency words	about after an another but called could don't girl good had her his home how laugh made make new next not now off over people put ran saw so some that them too took tree way were what will with
	Context words	bone broken chicken click clothes cushion groaned joke nobody notice princess silly still teeth things wig won't
Christmas Adventure	Year 2 High frequency words	again an be been but came did do don't good had have help here his home house just made many must new not old off put red so some them then there time too took tree want were what where your
	Context words	busy cheered Christmas computer crackers decorations December dinner disappointed Eve Father forget found given later lemonade most night nobody presents programme sorry thank tomorrow work
The Go-kart Race	Year 2 High frequency words	about an another back but called did don't down first good got had help her made make new not old one out put ran saw so there three time too took two what were will
	Context words	best brilliant broken Bullet coin crashed drive fast front notice plans race rusty Silver starter still third tossed upset worry
The Shiny Key	Year 2 High frequency words	about after be but called came down good had have here made must new or put ran saw so some that them these took tree very want what where were will your
	Context words	armchair beautiful bright dropped ear-ring gloomy locked missing magpie nest prince programme shiny soldiers sorry stolen suddenly thief thieves things thought toffee

HS

Teaching Notes

Contents

A Fright in the Night

Rotten Apples

The Laughing Princess

Christmas Adventure

The Go-kart Race

The Shiny Key

Introduction

The stories at Stage 6 continue the adventures of Biff, Chip, Kipper and friends. The magic key device enables the stories to incorporate adventure and fantasy within a safe setting. The introduction of new vocabulary and the sentence structures continue to be controlled in the stories, and key words from previous stages are frequently used.

At this level, it is still important to introduce the story through discussion, to enable children to read the texts with increasing confidence and independence. The sight vocabulary the children have gained in the earlier stages provides a platform for children to combine their knowledge of letter sounds and word meanings to interpret new words as they meet them in these stories. Words from the NLS high frequency word list are also used, so children can learn these words as sight vocabulary.

How to introduce the books

At Stage 6 it is still important to introduce the stories before independent reading. This will give the children sufficient information about the context and setting to enable them to read with confidence and independence.

Before reading the story, talk about the cover and the title. Read the back cover blurb and ask them to predict what the story is about. Go through the book together, looking at the pictures and talking about them. Point out and read any new context words that might prove difficult.

This booklet provides suggestions for using the books in group and independent activities. Prompts and ideas are provided for introducing and reading each book with a child or group of children. Suggestions are also provided for writing, speaking and listening and cross curricular links. You can use these suggestions to follow on from your reading, or use at another time.

Curriculum coverage chart

	Speaking and listening	Reading	Writing
A Fright in the Night			
NLS/NC	1d, 1e, 3a	W5, W6, W7, S1, S6, T6	T10
Scotland	Level A	Level A	Level A
N. Ireland	Activities: a, f, g Outcomes: a, b, c, d, e	Activities: a, b, c Outcomes: b, c, e, f, g	Outcomes: a, b, c
Wales	Range: 1, 2, 3 Skills: 1, 2, 3, 4	Range: 1, 2, 4, 5, 6 Skills: 1, 2	Range: 1, 2, 3, 4, 5 Skills: 1, 2, 4, 7, 8
Rotten Apples			
NLS/NC	1d, 4a	W4, S1, S3, S6, T3	T11
Scotland	Level A	Level A	Level A
N. Ireland	Activities: a, b, c, e, f Outcomes: a, b, c, d, e	Activities: a, b, c, e Outcomes: b, c, d, e, f	Outcomes: a, b, c, e
Wales	Range: 1, 2, 3, 5, 6 Skills: 1, 2, 3, 4, 5, 6	Range: 1, 2, 4, 5, 6 Skills: 1, 2	Range: 1, 2, 3, 4, 5 Skills: 1, 3, 7, 8
The Laughing Princess			
NLS/NC	1e, 2d	W1, W5, W6, S3, S5, T4	T10
Scotland	Level A	Level A	Level A
N. Ireland	Activities: a, e, f, g Outcomes: a, b, c, d, e	Activities: a, b, c, e, f, g Outcomes: b, c, d, e, f	Outcomes: a, b, c, d, f
Wales	Range: 1, 2, 3, 5 Range: 1, 2, 3, 4, 5	Range: 1, 2, 4, 5, 6 Skills: 1, 2	Skills: 1, 2, 3, 4, 5 Skills: 1, 2, 3, 5, 7, 8
Christmas Adventure			
NLS/NC	3a, 3b	W5, W6, W7, S3, T2, T5	T10
Scotland	Level A	Level A	Level A
N. Ireland	Activities: a, e, f, g Outcomes: a, b, c, d	Activities: a, b, c, f Outcomes: b, c, d, e, f	Outcomes: a, b, c, d
Wales	Range: 1, 2, 3 Skills: 1, 2, 3, 4, 5, 6	Range: 1, 2, 4, 5, 6 Skills: 1, 2	Range: 1, 2, 3, 4, 5, 7 Skills: 1, 4, 5, 7, 8
The Go-kart Race			
NLS/NC	W2, W8, S1, S3, T4	T17	1c, 1d, 1e
Scotland	Level A	Level A	Level A
N. Ireland	Activities: a, b, g Outcomes: a, b, c, d, e	Activities: a, b, c, e, f Outcomes: b, c, d, e, f	Outcomes: b, d
Wales	Range: 1, 2, 3 Skills: 1, 2, 3, 4	Range: 1, 2, 4, 5, 6 Skills: 1, 2	Range: 1, 2, 3, 4, 5, 7 Skills: 1, 2, 3, 5, 6
The Shiny Key			
NLS/NC	1d, 2d	W1, W4, S3, S4, T5	T11
Scotland	Level A	Level A	Level A
N. Ireland	Activities: a, e, f , g Outcomes: a, b, c, d, e	Activities: a, b, c, e Outcomes: b, c, e, f	Outcomes: a, c, e, i
Wales	Range: 1, 2, 3, 5 Skills: 1, 2, 4, 5, 6	Range: 1, 2, 4, 5, 6 Skills: 1, 2	Range: 1, 2, 3, 4, 5 Skills: 1, 2, 3, 4, 5, 7, 8

A Fright in the Night

Before reading

- Look at the cover with the children, and read the title together.
- Ask the children to read the back cover blurb and say what they think Biff and Chip will see at Gran's house.

During reading

- Ask the children to read the story. Praise and encourage them while they read, and prompt as necessary.
- Encourage the children to make use of the clues in the pictures to work out new words.
- If they struggle with the word "ghosts" on page 9, encourage them to read to the end of the page and predict a word that makes sense.

Observing Check that the children:

- ■ read the high frequency words on sight (W5/6)
- ■ use an awareness of grammar to work out new words (S1).

Group and independent reading activities

Text level work

Objective To discuss familiar story themes and link to own experience (T6).

- Discuss what Biff and Chip like about staying at Gran's house. Ask the children: *What do you like about your own house?*
- In pairs, ask the children to write a list of the things they like about their houses.

Observing Do the children discuss and collaborate their ideas with their partners?

Sentence level work

Objective To use a variety of simple organisational devices, e.g. arrows, to indicate sequences and relationships (S6).

You will need a copy of these sentences for each child, positioned randomly on the page:

Biff and Chip went to stay with Gran.
It was time for bed.
Biff put the sheet over her head.

Chip looked out of the window.
It is a ghost this time.
"I don't have ghosts," said Gran. "But I do have two monsters."

- Ask the children to read the sentences and link them by drawing arrows to show the order in which they come in the story.

Observing   Do the children need to refer to the book to find the sequence?

Word level work

Objective   To use word endings "–ed" (past tense) and "–ing" (present tense) to support their reading and spelling (W7).

- Read page 8 to the children, focusing on the verbs "loved" and "helped". Ask the children: *What is Biff doing?*
- Discuss how the word "help" can be changed by adding "–ed" and "–ing".
- Ask the children to look through the book and find all the verbs with "–ed" endings and re-write them so they end with "–ing".

Observing   Do the children understand that changing the verb ending also changes the tense?

Speaking and listening activities

Objectives   Focus on the main point (1d); include relevant detail (1e); take turns in speaking (3a).

- Sit with the children in a circle and ask each child to say one thing that describes Gran's house.
- Ask the children to name as many different sorts of buildings as they can think of that are used as homes.

Writing

Objective To use story structure to write about own experience in same/similar form (T10).

- Read the beginning of the story to the children and discuss how Biff and Chip went to stay with Gran.
- On the board write headings for the children to use in their own writing, based on the structure of the story, e.g. "Arriving"; "What the house is like"; "What I do first"; "What I do next"; "What I do last;" "How do I feel?"
- Ask the children to write about staying with a relative, or their best friend, and use the headings as a structure for writing their story.

Cross-curricular link
◀▶ Art & Design: Can buildings speak?

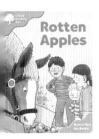

Rotten Apples

Before reading

- Look at the picture on the cover together, and ask the children to say what they think is happening.
- Ask them to read the title and the back cover blurb. Ask the children: *What sort of trouble do you think will happen?*

During reading

- Ask the children to read the story. Praise and encourage them while they read, and prompt as necessary.
- Encourage the children to follow the print with their eyes, only pointing when they have difficulty with a word.
- If children have difficulty reading contractions, e.g. "didn't", tell them to look for a familiar word within it and predict the rest of the word.

Observing Check that the children:

- predict words that make sense of the sentence if they have difficulty with a word (S1)
- take account of the punctuation, including commas and exclamation marks while reading (S3).

Group and independent reading activities

Text level work

Objective To be aware of the difference between spoken and written language through comparing oral recounts with text (T3).

- Ask the children to work with a partner. One child chooses an illustration in the story and covers up the text on that page. The other child says what sentences he/she would write to match the picture. The first child uncovers the text and the two children compare the differences between the text and the child's own sentences.
- Ask the children to swap roles and repeat the activity with a different illustration.

Observing Do the children use formal story language when describing what the picture shows?

Sentence level work

Objective To use a variety of simple organisational devices to indicate sequences and relationships (S6).

You will need a large sheet of paper for each child, with a "story path" leading from "The garden" to "The car park".

● Ask the children to draw and write the key events of the story along the "path" to show the order in which they happen.

Observing Do the children pick out key events showing cause and effect?

Word level work

Objective To investigate and classify words with the same sounds but different spellings (W4).

You will need these word cards: sum, maid, buy, sea, sore, no.

● Ask the children to read the words and look through the story to find and list words with the same sound but different spellings.
● Ask them to think of other words that sound the same but are spelt differently and write them down.

Observing Do the children understand how spelling affects meaning?

Speaking and listening activities

Objectives To focus on the main point (1d); use language and actions to explore and convey situations, characters and emotions (4a).

● Discuss the role the horse plays in Harry Smith's life. Can the children suggest other animals that work for humans?
● Ask some children to take the role of Harry Smith and describe what happened when he took his horse and cart to Biff's house. Tell them to use "when" and "because" in their sentences. Encourage the other children to ask questions about the events.

Cross-curricular link
◀▶ Citizenship: Animals and us

Writing

Objective To use language of time to structure a sequence of events (T11).

- Read page 20 to the children and discuss how "suddenly" and "Then" help the reader to understand the sequence.
- Discuss the picture on pages 20 and 21. Ask the children to work with a partner and explore what the policewoman is doing.
- Tell the children to write what happens when the policewoman comes over to the horse and cart.
- Scribe some of the children's suggestions on the board, and discuss how using temporal words and phrases, such as "meanwhile", "suddenly", "at first", "next", improves their accounts.

The Laughing Princess

Before reading

- Discuss the cover illustration, and ask the children to predict the setting of the story.
- Ask the children to read the title and the back cover blurb. Discuss what Kipper is holding and ask the children: *How do you think Kipper makes the princess laugh?*
- Look briefly through the illustrations to confirm the children's predictions.

During reading

- Ask the children to read the story. Praise and encourage them while they read, and prompt as necessary.
- Encourage the children to look carefully at the initial sounds and the picture clues to confirm any new words they see, e.g. on page 6 they should read the word as "notice", not "poster".

Observing Check that the children:

- read the familiar high frequency words with confidence (W5/6)
- pause at commas when reading "Biff made a funny face, but..." and other sentences with commas (S3).

Group and independent reading activities

Text level work

Objective To understand time and sequential relationships in stories (T4).

You will need these sentences from the story written as sentence strips or on word processing software:

First a girl told the king a joke.
Next a man dressed as a chicken.
Then the joke teeth went click, click, click.
Suddenly Kipper dropped the teeth.
A dog ran off with them.
The king fell over.
The teeth were broken.
At last the princess laughed and laughed.

- Mix up the sentences, and ask the children to sequence them in an order that makes sense, by arranging the strips, or dragging and dropping them into order on the computer.

Observing Do the children take account of the language of time to help them order the sentences?

Sentence level work

Objective To revise knowledge about other uses of capitalisation (S5).

- Discuss the notices in the illustrations on pages 6 and 7.
- Ask the children to explain why Monday and Tuesday begin with capitals.
- Ask them to write the days of the week for a poster to display in the classroom.

Observing Do the children know the days of the week and their order?
Do they write with care, correctly using upper and lower case letters?

Word level work

Objective To secure identification, spelling and reading of long vowel digraphs (W1).

- Write the words "joke" and "groaned" on the board, and ask the children to read the words and listen to the vowel sound.
- Ask the children to read through the book and collect the words that have the same vowel sound: no, glow, notice, over, bone, won't, window, so, home, nobody, go, know.
- Ask them to group the words according to their spelling patterns.

Observing Do the children recognise that "now" has a different sound from "glow"?

Speaking and listening activities

Objectives Include relevant detail (1e); listen to others' reactions (2d).

- Sit in a circle with the children, and ask them to each describe what they would do to make the princess laugh. The children can act this out in front of the group to see if they can make the other children laugh!

Writing

Objective To use story structure to write about own experience in same/similar form (T10).

- Discuss with the children the things that make them laugh.
- Scribe some of their ideas on the board, using this sentence as a model: "When I…it makes me laugh and laugh because…"
- Ask the children to write a description of something that has made them laugh recently, and use the structure of the sentence to help them.

Christmas Adventure

Before reading

- Look at the cover together and ask the children: *Where do you think the children are in this adventure? What do you think the "F" in the sign stands for?*
  Turn to pages 10 and 11. Does the writing on the boxes in the picture give you a clue?
- Ask them to read the back cover blurb and say what they think the story is about.
- Look briefly through the book to confirm the children's ideas.

During reading

- Ask the children to read the story. Praise and encourage them while they read, and prompt as necessary.
- Encourage the children to track the text with their eyes, and only point to words when they have difficulty.

Observing Check that the children:

- read high frequency words on sight (W5/6)
- use a variety of strategies to work out new words (T2).

Group and independent reading activities

Text level work

Objective To identify and discuss reasons for events in stories, linked to plot (T5).

- Ask the children to work with a partner. Tell each child to write down five questions about what happened in the story and to begin the questions with "Why did...?" and "What happened when...?"
- Tell the children to swap and answer their partner's questions.

Observing Do the children refer to the story to find causes and effects?

Sentence level work

Objective To recognise and take account of commas and exclamation marks (S3).

You will need to write these sentences, without punctuation, on the board:

The children were excited but Mum was hot and Dad was cross
He wanted the children to help but they didn't want to
That's funny said Chip

The children looked for Father Christmas but he was not there
Hooray said Wilf

- Tell the children the punctuation is missing from these sentences. Ask them to find the sentences in the story and re-write them, adding in the speech marks, exclamation marks and commas.

Observing Do the children notice that commas are used at the end of the direct speech?

Word level work

Objective To use word endings "–ed" (past tense) and "–ing" (present tense) to support their reading and spelling (W7).

- Write the word "watching" on the board, and talk about present tense verbs.
- Explain how adding "–ing" or "–ed" to the root word changes its tense.
- Write "have" on the board. Ask the children to suggest how to change it to "having". Talk about the need to omit the "e" from the root word.
- Ask the children to read the story and collect examples of verbs that drop the "e" from the root word when "–ing" is added.
- Can they add any other verbs that change in the same way?

Observing Are the children able to identify the root word of past tense verbs, e.g. took/take?

Speaking and listening activities

Objectives Take turns in speaking (3a); relate their contributions to what has gone on before (3b).

- Ask the children to look at the illustration on pages 10 and 11. Read the words written on the side of the boxes.
- Ask the children why they think the "I want" box has the most letters in it.
- Ask them to take turns to say how they think you should ask for a present and why.

Writing

Objective To use story structure to write about own experience in same/similar form (T10).

- Discuss with the children how to write a letter to Father Christmas. Model writing a letter as an example for them to follow.
- Remind the children that commas are used to punctuate a list of items.
- Ask the children to write their own letter to Father Christmas.

Cross-curricular link
◀▶ Religious education: Celebrations

The Go-kart Race

Before reading

- Look at the cover together, and ask the children to say what they think the story will be about.
- Ask them to read the title and the back cover blurb.
- Look briefly through the book to confirm the children's ideas.

During reading

- Ask the children to read the story. Praise and encourage them while they read, and prompt as necessary.
- Encourage the children to look for clues in the pictures to help them read new words.

Observing Check that the children:

- ■ are able to work out words with long vowel phonemes, e.g. "need", "paint", "wheels" (W2)
- ■ use the sense of the sentence to predict new words (S1)
- ■ note the sentences with exclamation marks and know to read them with expression (S3).

Group and independent reading activities

Text level work

Objective To understand time and sequential relationships in stories (T4).

- Ask the children to work with a partner. Tell each child to choose five key parts of the story and to write each as a sentence on a strip of paper.
- Once children have written all five sentences ask them to mix them up.
- The children then swap their sentences with their partner and sequence the new strips into the order in which they happen in the story.

Observing Are the children able to pick out significant incidents to re-tell the story?

Sentence level work

Objective To recognise and take account of commas and exclamation marks in reading aloud with appropriate expression (S3).

- In pairs, ask the children to read only the speech in the story. Each child reads alternate pages as they think the character would say it.

Observing Do the children recognise how punctuation tells them where speech starts and finishes?

Word level work

Objective To secure understanding and use of the terms "vowel" and "consonant" (W8).

- Ask the children to say which letters of the alphabet are vowels.
- Ask them to choose four pages from the book and collect words with two different vowels in them, e.g. "race", and three different vowels in them, e.g. "notice". Discuss and compare the words the children find.
- Ask them to point out the words that begin with a vowel.

Observing Do the children recognise that some words have one vowel sound made by two letters, e.g. "out"?

Speaking and listening activities

Objectives Organise what they say (1c); focus on the main point (1d); include relevant detail (1e).

You may need a reference book on making go-karts.

- Ask the children, in pairs, to discuss how they would make their own go-kart, what materials they would need and how they would decorate it.
- Ask the children to share their ideas with the rest of the group.
- Confirm the ideas by looking at the instructions in your reference book, if you are using one.

Writing

Objective   To use diagrams in instructions, e.g. drawing and labelling diagrams as part of a set of instructions (T17).

- Ask the children to look at the picture on page 5.
- Discuss how to write a set of instructions for making a go-kart.
- Together, write a list of what you need, and ask the children to suggest the steps to take. Scribe the instructions on the board.
- Ask the children to draw and label a diagram to use as part of these instructions.

Cross-curricular link
◀▶   Design and Technology: Vehicles

The Shiny Key

Before reading

- Look at the cover together and discuss what is happening. Ask the children: *Why has the bird got the key in its beak? Do you know what kind of bird it is?*
- Ask them to read the title and the back cover blurb and say what they think will happen in the story.

During reading

- Ask the children to read the story. Praise and encourage them while they read, and prompt as necessary.
- If the children struggle with the word "beautiful" help them by reading the word so they don't lose the sense of the story.

Observing Check that the children:

- read the long "ee" sound in "toffee" and the long "ie" sound in "magpie" (W1)
- read exclamations and questions with appropriate expression (S3).

Group and independent reading activities

Text level work

Objective To identify and discuss reasons for events in stories, linked to plot (T5).

- Discuss the events of the story and say to the children: *I wonder why that happened?*
- Choose children to sit in the "hot-seat" and take the role of Nadim. Encourage the other children to ask questions about what happened, beginning their questions with "why".

Observing Do the children ask questions that relate to cause and effect? Do the children answer the questions giving valid reasons for the events?

Sentence level work

Objective To re-read own writing for sense and punctuation (S4).

You will need to write these sentences on the board or on sentence strips:

Chip found the key.
Nadim cleaned the key.

The children were in a wood.
The soldiers took the children to the prince.
Suddenly, a magpie flew down.

- Ask the children to write two sentences after each one on the board, to continue the story.
- When they have finished, ask them to read all the sentences to check them for sense and use of correct punctuation.

Observing Do the children use other punctuation, as well as full stops?

Word level work

Objective To investigate and classify words with the same sounds but different spellings (W4)

- Write the word "toffee" on the board. Ask the children to say the final sound of the word.
- Ask them to look through the book and collect examples of other words with the same final sound: key, suddenly, sticky, shiny, gloomy, lady, tree, be, see, crossly, sorry.
- The children then group the words according to their spelling patterns.

Observing Can the children identify three different ways of spelling the long "ee" vowel sound?

Speaking and listening activities

Objectives Focus on the main point (1d); listen to other's reactions (2d).

- Sit with the children in a circle, and ask them to say whether it was fair or unfair of the soldiers to blame the children for stealing the ring.
- Ask the children to say whether they have been blamed for something they haven't done.
- Discuss whether the magpie knows what is right and what is wrong in the same way as humans do.

Cross-curricular link
◀▶ Citizenship: Choices

Writing

Objective   To use language of time to structure a sequence of events (T11).

- Discuss with the children the events of the story, and ask them to re-tell it using time connectives. Draw up a list of connectives from the children's suggestions.
- Ask the children to use words from the list to help them to describe what happened when the magpie flew down and took the magic key.

Oxford Reading Tree resources at this level

There is a range of material available at a similar level to these stories which can be used for consolidation or extension.

Stage 6

Teacher support
- Teacher's Handbook
- Take-Home Card for each story
- Storytapes
- Woodpeckers Photocopy Masters
- Group Activity Sheets Book 3 Stages 6–9
- ORT Games Stages 6–9

Further reading
- Woodpeckers Phonics Anthologies 2–5
- Playscripts Stages 6 & 7
- Fireflies Non-Fiction
- Fact Finders Units D and E
- Catkins and More Catkins Poetry

Electronic
- Clip Art
- Stage 6 & 7 Talking Stories
- ORT Online www.OxfordReadingTree.com
- Floppy and Friends

OXFORD
UNIVERSITY PRESS

Great Clarendon Street, Oxford OX2 6DP

Oxford University Press is a department of the University of Oxford. It furthers the University's objective of excellence in research, scholarship, and education by publishing worldwide in

Oxford New York

Auckland Bangkok Buenos Aires Cape Town Chennai
Dar es Salaam Delhi Hong Kong Istanbul Karachi Kolkata
Kuala Lumpur Madrid Melbourne Mexico City Mumbai Nairobi
São Paulo Shanghai Taipei Tokyo Toronto

Oxford is a registered trade mark of Oxford University Press in the UK and in certain other countries

© Oxford University Press 2003

The moral rights of the author have been asserted

Database right Oxford University Press (maker)

First published 2003

British Library Cataloguing in Publication Data

Data available

Cover illustrations Alex Brychta

Teacher's Notes: ISBN 0 19 8452330

10 9 8 7 6 5 4

Page make-up by IFA Design Ltd, Plymouth, Devon

Printed in Hong Kong